Landscape Quilts for Kids

Nancy Zieman and Natalie Sewell

© 2004 by Nancy Zieman and Natalie Sewell

Published by

700 East State Street • Iola, WI 54990-0001
715-445-2214 • 888-457-2873
www.krause.com

Our toll-free number to place an order or obtain
a free catalog is (800) 258-0929.

The following trademarked or registered company or product names appear in this book:
AppliqEase™ Lite, Big Foot®, Bubble Jet Set 2000®, Colorfast Printer Fabric™, Jacquard Inkjet Print on
Silk, Pellon® Polyester Fleece, Pellon® Wonder Under, Printer Treasure by Milliken, Quick Fix, Quilt
Sew Easy, Radio Flyer, Sewing With Nancy®, Sharp, Southern Belle, Templar®

Library of Congress Catalog Number: 2003117177

ISBN: 0-87349-859-3

Designer: Marilyn McGrane
Editor: Barbara Case
Illustrator: Laure Noe
Photographer: Dale Hall

Printed in the United States of America

Notes from Natalie and Nancy

Natalie and Nancy.

Over the last 12 years, I've made hundreds of landscape quilts. But they were complicated, intricate scenes. The question arose, "What kind of quilt should I make for a grandchild?" I wanted it to be personal and reflect his or her real interests. It occurred to me that I could simplify my landscape scenes by making them much more childlike and even depict the actual kids and their favorite animals.

Converting complicated landscape scenes required me to think like a child. Trees with many hues and intricate branches had to become big sticks with lollipop tops. Complicated groundcover had to turn into brightly flowered meadows. I could have animals wandering freely in meadows and could even depict the kids themselves playing happily in their favorite scenes.

When Nancy saw these quilts, she realized that this concept made sense for children everywhere. With her gift for educating, *Landscape Quilts for Kids* came to be. We have included enough tools and techniques for you to create a landscape quilt for your child and all children everywhere.

This has been a true labor of love. Like all grandmas, I think my grandchildren are very special and I've been delighted to be able to depict them and their interests in quilts for their rooms. Now you can do the same for your wonderful kids and grandkids.

Natalie

When I saw the first three landscape quilts Natalie was making for her grandchildren, I thought, "Wow, I'd like to make one for my nephews and nieces." Then I thought, "Wouldn't everyone like to make one?" Soon we taped a *Sewing With Nancy* television series about these quilts.

Traditionally every new TV series is accompanied by a 24-page booklet. And that 24-page booklet would have been fine if Natalie had stopped at three quilts! Once she got started, the ideas kept flowing. Soon, three quilts become six, then 10, and now 16! I knew that this topic would not fit into 24 pages. In addition to the 16 quilts, we had already created 24 pages of photo transfers featuring kids of every race and color, four seasons of clothing, and lots of accessories and animals.

It's been a joyous team effort. We hope you have as much enjoyment creating these quilts for the kids in your life.

Nancy

Dedication

To James, Rochel, Ben, Esther, Leah and Elijah. Thanks for the inspiration!

Chapter 1:
Getting Started

Chapter 2:
Animal
Landscapes

Contents

Chapter 1

Creating whimsical *Landscape Quilts for Kids* is much easier than it looks. Remember the way you drew as a child? First you drew the blue sky, then the green grass with flowers sticking up here and there. Next you added stick-straight tree trunks and lollipop leaves.

Now you can use the same process again. But this time, because you're cutting up fabric instead of coloring with crayons, the effect will look much more sophisticated. The secret is in choosing an inspiring snapshot, selecting the right fabrics, and following some simple landscape quilting techniques.

The "Anna" quilt may seem complicated at first glance but, in fact, the sky is a single piece of fabric, the groundcover is another single piece (with a few optional flowers added), the trees are brown fabric strips, and the leaves are all from the same piece of foliage fabric. All of the kids and even their accessories can be transferred from the pages in the back of this book to printer fabric sheets. And, depending on how densely you choose to machine quilt, you can make a quilt like this one for your child or grandchild in very little time.

Getting Started

Photo

Once you've decided which child or children you're going to make the quilt for, your next job is choosing the subject matter. Of course you are welcome to recreate any of the kids' quilts in this book but you may want to incorporate personal experiences or scenes as well.

Your own family photo albums make the best source material. But be flexible. If a photo seems too complicated or contains irrelevant details, simply eliminate those details. On the other hand, feel free to add whatever whimsical element you think your child would like to include. Elephants can roam

Inspirations

through flower gardens, and trees can bear huge red apples if you want them to.

Remember that the photo is simply a starting place for your scene. Depending on what you like and what fabrics you have in your stash, you can change the scene any way you choose.

Fabric Selection

Choosing fabrics for a child's wall quilt will help to set the mood for the whole room. The following tips may make your selection easier.

Sky fabrics.

Sky Fabrics

Sky fabrics play a central role in most of the children's quilts in this book. A pale blue sky means a sunny day, whatever the season, and sets up a sunny mood for kids and animals at play. So, of course, almost all of our quilts have blue skies. The only exceptions are "Halloween," "Peace" (a Christmas scene), and "Horses in the Snow" – all scenes that take place in early evening, before bedtime, when the sky is getting dark.

Sky fabric is also important because it's the biggest single fabric in the quilt scene, and thus becomes the background fabric. We usually cut the sky fabric the size of the finished quilt and build all the other elements on it. To make our skies more interesting we often choose fabrics with many shades of pale blue and tinges of yellow, purple, and white to suggest clouds and sun streaks.

Note from NATALIE

Hand-dyed fabrics (sold by the piece, not the yard) make wonderfully colorful skies and set a cheery tone for the whole quilt. Sold at special quilt shops, through direct mail, or through the Internet, they are a great choice because of their irregular texture.

Foliage and Floral Fabrics

Look for small-scale leaves, flowers, and grasses. Many fabrics include all three, which saves you the trouble of adding one to the other (for example, clusters of flowers to grasses). We believe no fabric is too colorful or corny for a child's landscape quilt, as long as the scale is appropriate for the scene.

Foliage and floral fabrics.

Snow Fabrics

To make snow, look for white, gray, or cream colored fabric with enough texture to create the illusion of drifts and shadows. As with any landscape fabric, never choose a solid color.

Snow fabrics.

Tree and Fence Fabrics

Commercially made wood-grain fabrics are readily available in most fabric shops. Textured light and dark grays and browns also make good tree trunks or fences, especially when shaded with fabric markers (see page 12). Again, avoid choosing solid colors. We tend to choose dark wood colors with pale blue sky and light wood-grain prints with night skies to make the trees more visible.

Tree and fence fabrics.

Conversational Prints

Although we've made many images of toys, pets, hobbies, and accessories available to you in the back of the book to transfer to printer fabric sheets, don't overlook the many enchanting conversational prints that abound in fabric stores. Cowboy hats, trucks, ballet shoes, dolls, teddy bears, sports equipment, etc. are often scaled just right to add to your child's scene.

Above: Boy's conversational prints.
Right: Girl's conversational prints.

Tools and Notions

As with any sewing or quilting project, *Landscape Quilts for Kids* requires specific tools and notions. The list is short, but important.

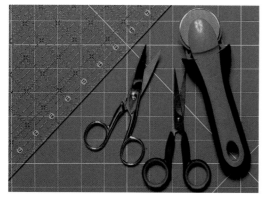

Cutting tools.

Cutting Tools

A 4" to 5" scissors with extremely sharp points is crucial for landscape quilting. Because cutting fabric into little pieces will be one of your main activities, finding a sharp scissors that is also comfortable to your hand is essential.

The cutting trio of a rotary cutter, mat, and ruler will be used primarily when squaring the quilt top, cutting borders, and cutting backing fabrics. Make certain that the cutter has sharp blades.

Glue stick.

Glue Sticks

Gluing is a key step in creating a landscape quilt. You'll need several paper or craft glue sticks for each quilt top. Test the glue by applying a consistent layer on a scrap of fabric. If the glue does not glide easily on the fabric, try another brand.

Fabric Markers

Fabric markers add depth and character to landscape designs. Choose markers with acid-free, nontoxic, permanent ink. We use them to highlight and shade tree trunks and grasses, or to change the color of leaves or flower petals.

A white correction pen, such as Quick-Fix, as featured in the photo, is useful for adding light shading to dark trees. This "landscape" notion is found at office supply stores.

Fabric markers.

Note from NANCY

Use a glue stick designed for gluing paper, not fabric! (A fabric glue stick is too sticky for this process.) You can find paper glue sticks in office supply stores rather than in fabric stores. The glue holds the fabric in place temporarily (that is, until you get a chance to sew it down on the background fabric). And it does not affect your sewing machine in any way.

Thread and Needles

Use a clear or transparent nylon or polyester thread for the free-motion quilting technique. The clear thread blends in with the fabric, eliminating the need to change thread colors when stitching on various fabrics. Use the clear thread as the top thread; choose a bobbin thread that matches your background fabric. To prevent having the bobbin thread poke through to the top layer, especially on all those pale blue skies, we suggest using a lightweight thread in the bobbin (such as a 50-wt. or even a 60-wt. thread).

Experiment with needle selection. Because we want the needle holes to be as small as possible around the kids' and animals' faces and limbs, we generally use a sharp needle, 70/10 size or a universal needle, size 70. Also, printer fabric sheets tend to be very dense and show needle holes easily. If your thread breaks, switch to a metallic or Metalfil needle that has a longer eye.

Clear thread.

Specialty Presser Feet

Many machines include a darning foot in the machine's accessory box. These feet are generally clear, allowing you to see where you're going and also where you've been. The feet are designed with a shorter shank height, allowing you to freely move the fabric under the foot area while providing sufficient surface contact with the fabric.

Available separately is a Big Foot, a giant darning foot with a larger "foot" area, providing a greater area of surface contact.

One style of darning foot.   *The Big Foot.*

Safety Pins

Choose size #1 safety pins for pinning the quilt layers together. There are two options in safety pins: the traditional straight pins or curved pins that are designed for easier insertion in the fabric.

Hoops or Grips

Landscape quilts are stitched in two phases: 1) free-motion machine stitching the elements to the background fabric, and 2) free-motion quilting the top, batting, and backing layers together. We recommend that you use *one* of the following hoops or grips when free-motion stitching.

Rubber fingers, used by office staff and available at office supply stores, allow you to move the fabric with ease while free-motion stitching. Wear the fingers on your index and middle fingers and thumbs.

Quilting gloves with coated fingertips keep you in control of your quilting while reducing resistance and drag on the fabric. Most quilting gloves are made of breathable fabric with nylon and polyurethane fingertip coating.

Quilt Sew Easy, a flexible hoop that sits on the top of the quilt, has a foam underside that allows you to hold the fabric with tight control, as if you were holding a steering wheel. You can then reposition it by simply lifting the hoop to another area of the quilt.

Hoops and grips.

Landscape Basics

There are basic techniques that are common to many of the landscape quilts featured in this book. Rather than repeating these directions every time a quilt is detailed, we will refer you back to this section. The basics are:

- cutting
- gluing
- making transfers of *Landscape Kids*
- making alphabet appliqués
- using digital photos
- machine stitching the quilt top
- squaring up the quilt top
- auditioning and adding borders

Cutting

Cutting is key to landscape quilting. There are three unique ways to cut fabrics for *Landscape Quilts for Kids* – we call them "messy," "fussy," and "tree" cutting!

Messy cutting is used primarily for foliage and groundcover. When you do messy cutting, forget everything you've ever learned about cutting. Cut as poorly as possible, jagging in and out to make rough edges. The secret is to cut badly – hence the name messy cutting.

Fussy cutting is used to cut out the shapes from the conversational prints, plus leaves and flowers that are relatively close-up. You'll be following the lines of the printed motifs in the fabric as you cut. This will take some time!

Messy cutting.

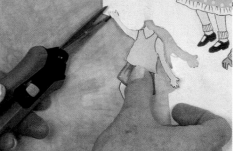

Fussy cutting.

Tree cutting is done with a rotary cutter and mat. But don't use a ruler, cut free form! Vary the trunk width to add more interest. Rough cut the bottom of the tree trunk to make it look like it's growing out of the grass or snow.

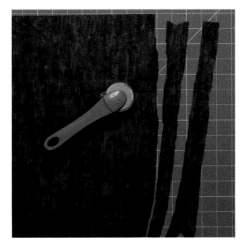

Tree cutting.

Gluing

Use a paper glue stick to position the messy and fussy cut pieces to the background fabric. Place the cutout fabric motif right side down on a large scrap of Pellon fleece batting. The batting keeps the fabric motif from shifting, protects your worktable from glue, and allows you to apply a consistent layer of glue from a paper/craft glue stick over the entire back of the fabric piece, extending over the fabric edges.

Apply a consistent layer of glue.

Note from NATALIE

This glue is traditionally used for paper, so a little dab won't do! You need to apply glue over the entire outer edge of the fabric or it won't stay in place when it's positioned on the background. We've noticed that many beginning landscape quilters tend to skimp on the amount of glue they use and feel very frustrated when the pieces they positioned so carefully fly off as they move the quilt top to the sewing machine.

Adding a likeness of your child to his or her quilt is what makes this technique special. On pages 80 to 90 you'll find a wide variety of kids' faces and hair styles, many choices of clothing for all seasons, and special accessories including toys, tools, pets, and wild animals that can be easily transferred to fabric with the help of printer fabric sheets and a color copier or printer.

For example, let's say you'd like to create a winter landscape that depicts your little pony-tailed redheaded girl. Simply select a likeness of her in the back of the book along with your favorite snowsuit and snow accessories. After transferring the head, snowsuit body, and accessories onto fabric printer sheets, you'll be able to fussy cut the head shape and body style. Here are the steps for transferring these images to fabric.

Choosing Printer Fabric Sheets

There are two types of printer fabric sheets. You can buy either premade, precut sheets, or you can make your own printer fabric. Choose the method that best fits your needs.

Using Premade Printer Fabric Sheets

If you like to get things done quickly, easily, and are willing to spend a little extra money, this method of transferring the *Landscape Kids* likeness is your best bet. These printer fabric sheets (Colorfast Printer Fabric, Printer Treasure by Milliken, and Inkjet Print on Silk by Jacquard) are ready to use the minute you open the package. Simply place the sheets into your inkjet copier or printer.

Printer fabric sheets.

- The printer fabric doesn't require any special preparation, heat transfer, or mirror imaging.
- Printer fabric sheets have a paper backing, allowing the fabric sheets to be fed through a computer.

Making Your Own Printer Fabric Sheets

If you plan to transfer a lot of images, making your own printer fabric sheets is an economical choice. Start with a tight weave, high fiber count fabric such as Southern Belle broadcloth and transform it into printer fabric. Your fabric will remain soft, with true color results, making it perfect for landscape quilts.

1. Cut 12" crosswise strips of the Southern Belle broadcloth. Subcut the strips into 9" x 12" rectangles, sections that are slightly larger than a standard 8½" x 11" piece of paper. It is easier to handle individual rectangles than to work with large yardage.

2. Thoroughly soak 100% cotton fabric in Bubble Jet Set 2000 for five minutes. Use any kind of container for soaking, such as a flat pan, glass casserole dish, or a bowl.

3. Let the fabric air dry. Do not wring the solution out of the fabric, let it drip back into the pan. Hang the fabric to dry.

4. Iron the dry sheets until they are completely smooth. Iron them onto freezer paper, meeting the wrong side of the fabric to the shiny side of the freezer paper.

Soak the fabric in Bubble Jet Set 2000.

5. Trim the sheets to 8½" x 11", using the copy paper template. This clear acrylic template is the perfect size for cutting photo transfer sheets for use in printers and copiers.

Trim the fabric sheets to 8½" x 11".

Transferring the Images

There are several ways to transfer images to fabric printer sheets. Choose the method that best fits your needs based on the type of equipment and software you own.

Using an Inkjet Color Printer

Printing your images to printer fabric sheets using an inkjet color copier is the quickest and easiest method.

1. Position the book on the copier glass with the right side down.
2. Print onto regular paper first to make sure the book is positioned correctly and you're not cutting off any parts of the images.
3. Load one sheet of printer fabric into the paper tray so copying occurs on the fabric side of the sheet.
4. Copy onto the fabric. Allow sufficient time to dry.
5. Remove the backing from the fabric.
6. Press with a dry iron to set the ink.

Use your printer to copy images.

Note from NATALIE

Not all of us have inkjet color copiers at home. Use the services of specialty office stores and libraries that make color copies for a small fee.

Using a Computer, Scanner, and Inkjet Printer

If you have a scanner along with your computer, you can scan the *Landscape Kids* images to your computer. That way you can use your photo edit program to select a higher quality print setting (with higher resolution), giving you more control over your finished product.

If you wish to reuse certain images or want to regroup elements from several pages onto one page to reduce the amount of printing you'll be doing, simply scan the images from the book directly to your computer's document file. Then you can rearrange and print them as often as you like.

1. Place the open book on the glass plate of the scanner with the image of the *Landscape Kids* facing down. Close the lid.
2. Scan the image, following the manufacturer's instructions.
3. Load one sheet of printer fabric into the paper tray so the printing occurs on the fabric side of the sheet.
4. Print and allow the ink to dry.
5. Remove the backing from the fabric.
6. Press with a dry iron to set the ink.

Note from NANCY

The instructions on the premade printer fabric sheets tell you to "rinse the fabric in cool water." Since these quilts are raw-edged wall hangings, not actual bed quilts that will be laundered, you can skip this step.

Making Alphabet Appliqués

Kids love to see their name in print, or in this case, in fabric. Many of the quilts in Chapter 3 feature 3" letters in either a stylized or block font. These letters, which are already mirror-imaged, are ready to be traced onto a paper-backed fusible web such as Pellon Wonder Under or AppliqEase Lite. Here's how to make alphabet appliqués.

1. Trace the mirror-imaged appliqué letters onto the paper side of the fusible web, leaving ¼" between them.

2. Fuse the letters to the wrong side of the appliqué fabric. If the letters will be cut from different fabrics, roughly cut out the letters to separate them from the original tracing.

3. After fusing, carefully cut out the fused letters, following the traced lines.

4. Peel away the paper backing and position the letters on the quilt.

Use Alphabet Appliqués to spell your child's name.

Note from NATALIE

Rather than making Alphabet Appliqués, consider purchasing 3" felt craft letters. This photo shows both purchased and "make-your-own" versions. The purchased letters are available at many craft stores and most often come in primary colors.

Felt craft letters and "make-your-own" letters.

Using Digital Photos

Rather than using the *Landscape Kids* images, you can use actual photos of children for your scene. This process might take a little planning and time, but the finished quilt will be treasured for a lifetime.

1. Take digital photos of your children. Snap several views, if possible.
2. Import the photos to your picture file.
3. Analyze the photos, looking specifically at the outline of your child. Ask yourself if the child could be cut out of the photo easily. For example, wisps of wind-blown hair are hard to cut around without making the child look unnatural. If you can, avoid cutting out profiles. It's difficult at best to cut delicate facial images accurately.
4. Either enlarge or reduce the photo so the child is the correct size for the quilt. Follow your computer software's instructions.
5. Print the photo onto the fabric side of the transfer sheet as described on page 17.

Print out digital photos from your computer.

Note from NANCY

Digital images of your pets are perfect additions to a landscape scene. Consider taking shots of the pet when it's sitting calmly! It is much easier to photograph and cut out a sitting dog or cat than one on the run!

Machine Stitching the Quilt Top

As you design your landscape quilt, you are gluing your fabric pieces to your background fabric. The glue temporarily holds the various quilt elements together and allows you to reposition them as you choose. However, once you are satisfied with your design, you will need to machine stitch the pieces to the background fabric to keep them in place.

Setting Up Your Sewing Machine for Free-Motion Stitching

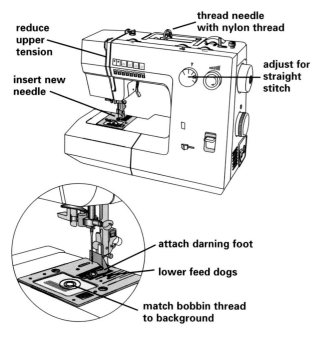

reduce upper tension

thread needle with nylon thread

insert new needle

adjust for straight stitch

attach darning foot

lower feed dogs

match bobbin thread to background

1. Lower the feed dogs. (Check your owner's manual if you are not sure of how to make this adjustment.)

2. Reduce the upper tension slightly. This adjustment varies from machine to machine.

3. Insert a new universal or sharp needle. Test your needle on your fabric to make sure it makes the smallest hole possible, and adjust your needle size accordingly. Some fabrics are denser and do better with a smaller needle.

4. Thread the needle with clear nylon thread.

5. Match the bobbin thread to the background color. If you can't decide between several colors, always choose the one that's slightly darker. Consider using a lighter weight thread, such as a 50 or 60 wt. to decrease the likelihood of your bobbin thread poking through to the front of the quilt. Don't use nylon thread in the bobbin.

6. Adjust the machine for a straight stitch.

7. Attach a specialty presser foot such as a darning or Big Foot.

Machine Stitching Around Shapes

1. Place the fabric under the presser foot and lower the presser foot to the darning or sewing position. The foot will slightly "glide" above the fabric.

2. Place your hands evenly on both sides of the needle, gently holding the quilt top in place. Use rubber fingers, a Quilt Sew Easy hoop, or quilting gloves as described on page 13.

3. Guide the fabric with your hands. Since the feed dogs are lowered, you, not your machine, will be controlling the fabric.

4. Move the fabric at an even speed under the presser foot area.

5. Stitch along the cut edges just enough to anchor the pieces firmly in place. If you stay close to the edges, you will not have to remove this "basting" later.

Machine stitch down the edges of the shapes.

Note from NANCY

Don't feel you have to cover every little edge with stitching. That step will be taken care of later in the machine quilting process. This step assures that the pieces won't fall off the quilt and your design will stay intact.

Squaring Up the Quilt Top

It's important to make sure your quilt top is a perfect rectangle before adding borders. Unlike most pieced quilts, landscape quilts have no horizontal or vertical lines to guide you as you try to trim your quilt top. Take time to do this accurately since it will determine how your finished quilt will look on the wall. It won't lie flat unless it's a perfect rectangle.

1. Steam iron the entire quilt top, pressing on the wrong side to prevent melting the nylon threads.

2. If puckers appear, flatten them with the steam iron or break the threads with your seam ripper and flatten the area with more steam.

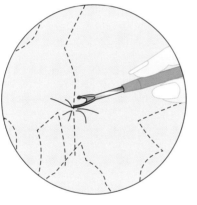

3. Fold the quilt top in half, meeting the top and lower edges.

4. Place the quilt top on a cutting mat, aligning the fold with one of the marked lines on the mat. Using a ruler and a rotary cutter, square the top and lower edges, making certain you're cutting parallel to the fold.

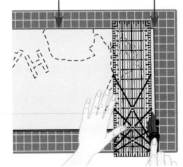

5. Unfold the quilt top and refold it in the opposite direction, meeting the side edges. Trim the side edges, again cutting parallel to the fold.

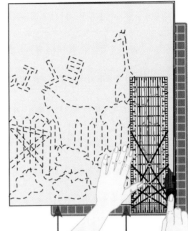

6. Unfold the quilt top and use a large square ruler to check that each corner is square. If necessary repeat the folding and trimming process until all the corners measure a perfect right angle.

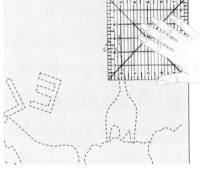

7. Check and recheck the "squareness" of the quilt top by measuring it from top to bottom, left to right, and corner to corner.

8. Steam the back of the quilt top with your iron. Press from the wrong side to flatten and stabilize the quilt top.

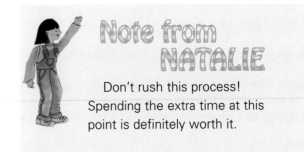

Note from NATALIE

Don't rush this process! Spending the extra time at this point is definitely worth it.

Auditioning Borders

Borders are to quilts as mats are to pictures, directing attention to the scene itself. You may want to choose a more whimsical border for a child's quilt than you would for a grown-up quilt, since it will probably hang in a less formal room of the house if not in the child's bedroom itself. We've chosen to border some of our kids' quilts with polka dots, plaids, checks, and flowers. Take time to audition some playful alternatives for border fabric.

Create playful borders for kids quilts.

Audition border fabrics.

Audition border fabric by folding it to a narrow width. Pin it alongside the quilt top. Decide which border best fits the mood of the quilt.

Adding Borders

1. Cut borders ½" wider than the desired finished width of the border. If using an inner border, cut strips 1" wide.

2. Stitch the inner borders to the outer borders with ¼" seam allowances. Press the seams toward the outer borders.

3. Cut two lengths a minimum of 8" longer than the top and bottom measurement of the quilt.

4. Cut two lengths a minimum of 8" longer than the side measurement of the quilt.

5. Pin the borders to the sides of the quilt top, right sides together.

6. Place a mark on the side borders ¼" from each corner of the quilt top.

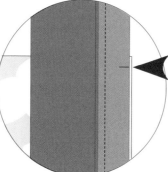

7. Stitch from mark to mark using a ¼" seam allowance.

8. Repeat, pinning and stitching the borders to the top and bottom of the quilt, again stopping the stitching ¼" from each corner and allowing 3" to 4" extensions at each end.

12. Stitch along the press mark, sewing to the point of the miter. Trim the seam allowances to ¼".

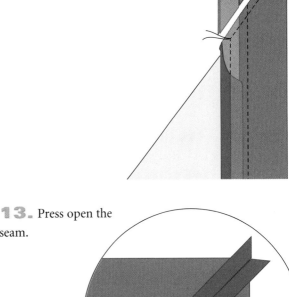

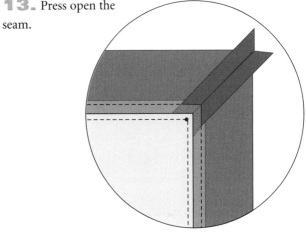

9. Form the miters, working with one corner at a time. Press the borders right side out to the finished position.

13. Press open the seam.

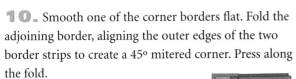

10. Smooth one of the corner borders flat. Fold the adjoining border, aligning the outer edges of the two border strips to create a 45° mitered corner. Press along the fold.

11. Pin the borders together at the mitered edge. Fold back the quilt top, exposing the wrong side and the press mark.

14. Repeat, mitering each corner.

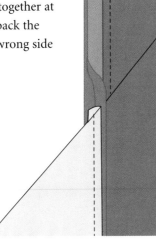

Chapter 2
Animal Landscapes

Fanciful animal quilts are easy to make and children of all ages love them. Perhaps your children or grandchildren love horses, or are infatuated with zebras or panda bears. You can create a special landscape quilt that reflects that interest. These scenes can be created with only four to six fabrics . . . sky, shrubbery, groundcover, and some lovable critters.

Fabric

Many quilts in this chapter, such as "Zebras" featured on the preceding pages, came to be because of the irresistible fabric choices available today. By the time you read this book, there will be even more choices to inspire you. Use what's currently available at your local fabric store or, if you're a collector like we are, raid your personal stash.

Inspirations

When choosing animal fabrics, ignore the color of the background fabric since you will be cutting out the animals and discarding the rest. If you choose animals from two or more prints, make certain that they are compatible both in size and style. If you can, cut them out and try them next to each other. A cartoon-styled tiger, for example, will look odd next to a realistic elephant.

Panda Bear Picnic

Let yourself fall in love with some of the new juvenile conversational print fabrics. That's what happened to us when we saw a new panda bear fabric. Once we cut out the bears and arranged them, the idea for a picnic seemed inevitable. A similar quilt could be made featuring any animals that appeal to you.

The background fabric is a green foliage pattern. The leaves are not botanically correct bamboo. Combine the foliage with grass, a tablecloth, a honey pot, and half a dozen pandas, and presto – the scene is complete.

Selecting Fabrics

Once you've found your panda bears, the next step is to select a background and groundcover fabric. Don't worry about botanical accuracy. Anything resembling bamboo will do for the panda bears. Here are some guidelines for choosing fabrics.

• Make sure the background fabric you select has at least five different hues, ranging from light to dark. Otherwise it will look like a solid from a distance and will flatten the mood of your design. At the same time, the background can't be so busy that it interferes with the panda bears themselves.

• Choose a print resembling groundcover. Pay special attention to the scale of the print, making certain it is proportionate to the bears.

"Panda Bear Picnic" fabric array.

• Use whatever fabrics you like for the tablecloth, honey pots, and basket. You may prefer to have the bears feast on something besides bamboo, or, who knows, play a game of cards instead. Of course, you are welcome to use our ideas and templates.

Creating the Scene

1. Cut the background fabric the size of the finished quilt. This quilt measures 12" x 22".

2. Cut a strip of grass fabric approximately one-third the width of the finished quilt. Messy cut along one edge.

3. Glue the back of the grass fabric liberally and position it along the lower edge of the bamboo background.

Make the background.

Place the panda bears.

4. Cut out the number of panda bears desired for your scene. We used six. Usually there are only three to five different animals in any given fabric. You will have to cut duplicates.

5. Glue and position the bears on the background fabric. Change the position or angle of the duplicate animals to make them look unique.

6. Add the picnic elements. The templates of a honey pot, basket, and tablecloth are pictured on page 75.

Note from NATALIE

In this fabric there are only five varieties of bears. To make the sixth bear look different, we've leaned one of the bears against its neighbor. It is amazing what canting an animal or tucking one behind another will do to make two identical animals look different from one another. If you'd like to make this quilt larger than ours, feel free to do so. Remember to cut out enough animals to make the scene look complete if you make it bigger.

Tilt the identical panda bear.

Stitching and Squaring the Quilt Top

1. Machine stitch around the shapes. Refer to the directions on page 20.
2. Square the quilt top. See the directions on page 21.

Auditioning and Adding Borders

Audition border fabrics by folding them to a narrow width (2" or 3" wide) and pinning them alongside the quilt top. (You don't want to cut a strip until you know for sure you want to use it.) As you're auditioning, think about mood as well as color. A child's quilt warrants a playful border.

1. Cut the border strips. Since we've made this quilt quite small, we've chosen to use narrow 2½" borders.

2. Add the borders. See the directions on page 22 to 23.

Audition border options.

Note from NATALIE

If you can't find animals you like in a conversational print, consider using the animals from the back of the book (pages 76 to 79) for your quilt design. The koala bear, combined with a few of the other animals from these pages, would work here. Or you could use just koalas. Print several, cut them out, and then tilt a few or change their coloration with a fabric marker so they don't look identical.

Horse Landscapes

Horses are a hot topic these days. In our two families alone, we have two passionate horse lovers... a grandson, age three, and a niece, age 13, who are equally in love with these majestic creatures.

We found such a wide variety of horse fabrics that we couldn't resist making three different horse quilts for you to choose from, featuring big, middle-sized, and little horses. In the following pages, you'll find these fabrics in three unique quilts. Make certain that the scale of the foliage and groundcover fabric works with the size of the animals in your fabric.

Note from NATALIE

The biggest horses are from pillow-panel yardage that I found on a clearance table. I knew I would never make throw pillows, but could certainly use the horse images in a landscape quilt for my grandson. Once I cut out the majestic horses, I threw away the rest of the yardage.

Horses in the Snow

This winter scene featuring wild horses at a full gallop would be a welcome sight in any room of your home, not just the kids' rooms. We chose the largest scale of horse print featured above for this animal landscape. You need only a few fabrics to create this dramatic quilt.

Selecting Fabrics

1. Select a dark navy for the background fabric. We used a navy hand-dyed fabric for the cold, winter sky. An attractive commercial fabric such as a navy or royal blue batik would be another effective choice. Make sure your winter sky fabric has mottled hues and that you avoid using solid colors.

2. Choose a multi-hued light print for the snow fabric. Snow rarely appears as a solid white. It always has shadows of gray, blue, and cream, depending on the light in the sky.

3. Choose a lighter tree fabric when using a dark sky so that it shows up. Our tree fabric has shades of gray to brown.

Note from NANCY

The tree-bark fabric in the photo is folded with the wrong side of the fabric up. With many fabric prints you have two shade options: the actual right side and the "other" right side.

"Horses in the Snow" fabric array.

Create the background and add trees.

Highlight the legs and hooves.

Note from NATALIE

On the original fabric these horses were depicted in a summer scene. After cutting out the manes and tails, some of the green background of the original fabric appeared on the horses. We used a black fabric marker to camouflage the green, transforming the horses from a summer to a winter scene with a few strokes of a pen.

Note from NANCY

Notice that there is no border on this quilt, only a binding. We think the simple binding gives the quilt a contemporary look. Feel free to finish your quilt any way you like …add a border, a double border, or skip it altogether and just add binding.

Creating the Scene

1. Cut the sky background fabric the size of the finished quilt. This background measures 34" x 20".

2. Cut a strip of snow fabric approximately one-third to one-half the width of the finished quilt. Messy cut the top of the snow, creating a gentle hill. The uneven terrain adds interest to the simple scene. For cutting guidelines, see page 14.

3. Glue and position the snow fabric to the lower edge of the background fabric. For gluing guidelines, see page 15.

4. Cut two trees from the tree fabric. Vary the width of the trunks to add interest. Cut the bottom of the tree trunks jagged to make the base of the tree look snow-covered. Glue and position the trees to the background.

5. Cut branches from thin strips of the tree fabric. When positioning the branches on the fabric, give the branches "elbows" rather than curves. Glue the branches on the fabric.

6. If the tree trunks are too dark against the background, lighten one side with a white marker or correction pen.

7. Fussy cut the large horses. Glue and position them to the design, overlapping the horses to add a sense of depth. If the horses are very large, don't feel obligated to use three in the scene – feature two, or even just one.

8. Highlight the legs and hooves of the horses with a white correction pen to give the illusion of snow flying.

Stitching and Squaring the Quilt Top

1. Machine stitch around the shapes. Refer to page 20 for instructions.

2. Square the quilt top. See the directions on page 21.

Herd of Winter Horses

T he same scene – white snow and dark sky make up the background for these horses but the scale is much smaller. We've also added fir trees, choosing a multi-shaded green fabric. You can create this design by following the directions for "Horses in the Snow" with these additional steps.

Use a correction marker to distinguish one tree from another.

Creating the Scene

1. Instead of making birch trees, cut out several fir trees using the template on page 75. We used seven fir trees in our design. Slightly vary the size of the template if you wish to make different sizes of trees. Position the trees in the design, overlapping them a little and using a correction marker to distinguish one tree from another.

2. Fussy cut numerous horses. We used 14 here to create the illusion of a real herd. Glue and position them on the snow. If you use this many horses, you will inevitably be duplicating some of them. To make them look varied, simply change some of their leg positions or use a dark fabric marker or a correction marker to change the coloration of the look-alikes. Sometimes you can partially hide one of the horses behind another to create a sense of variety.

3. Add a border to the quilt. Refer to pages 22 to 23 for border techniques.

Horses Out to Pasture

Once you understand the general concept of creating landscape scenes that feature animals, you can change the seasons to suit your fancy. We used the mid-size horse print to depict prancing horses out to pasture.

"Horses Out to Pasture" fabric array.

Selecting Fabrics

1. Select a spring or summer sky fabric for the background fabric. We used a hand-dyed fabric but there are equally attractive commercial fabrics to simulate a summer sky. Look for subtle hues in the light blues and yellows.

2. Choose a groundcover fabric that depicts grass or pasture in proportion to the size of the horses. In this case, the grasses have multiple hues of green.

3. Include several clumps of small-scale foliage to highlight the ground-cover. We purposely chose a variety of green foliage prints to add contrast.

Note from NATALIE

The step-by-step photos on page 37 feature a late summer scene with dried grasses, instead of lush green foliage. However, the finished quilt and the fabrics above feature a spring pasture. You can change the season simply by changing the color of the grasses, leaves, and even the sky.

Creating the Scene

1. Cut the sky background fabric the size of your finished quilt. Our background measures 33" x 18".

2. Messy cut the top of the groundcover. The uneven terrain creates an interesting simple scene. The grass-type fabric should cover one-fourth to one-third of the lower edge of the quilt.

3. Glue and position the groundcover fabric to the background fabric. For gluing guidelines, see page 14.

4. Messy cut the foliage fabric to resemble shrubbery. Remember to check the wrong side of the fabric to see if that lighter shade could add highlights to the scene.

5. Glue the shrubbery pieces, then tuck them behind the groundcover fabric.

6. Fussy cut the horses. Cut out a number that will comfortably fit the scale of the design. Usually there are three or four horse positions per fabric. If desired, cut several of the same horse.

7. Change the look of identical horses by shading their markings darker or lighter with fabric markers or correction pens.

8. Glue and position the horses on the scene.

Stitching and Squaring the Quilt Top

1. Machine stitch around the shapes. Refer to the directions on page 20.

2. Square the quilt top. See the directions on page 21.

Create the background.

Create a bucking bronco.

Note from NATALIE

You can alter a horse's position by simply tipping him on his hind legs and changing the position of his front legs a little. My three-year-old grandson loves bucking broncos, which prompted me to create this quilt for him. A little manipulation of the horse's position turned a duplicate horse into a bucking one.

Zebras

Zebras may be grumpy, but they are graphically beautiful! This animal landscape depicts five zebras calmly eating flowers in a garden. How and why they got there we'll leave to the kids to figure out.

You can create this design by following the directions for "Horses Out to Pasture," page 36. The only significantly different step is Patching Animals, detailed below.

Patching Animals

The animal print fabric we used did not have complete animals, but because of our cutting and gluing tricks, this was not a problem. Even though you may not be making a zebra quilt with this fabric, you might find our technique for patching animals to be a useful tool in the "art" of making animal landscape quilts.

1. Cut out the shape of the animal as whole as possible.

2. Cut a "patch" from another like animal from the same fabric. Glue the patch in position.

3. Use fabric markers, if necessary, to blend the patched fabric pieces.

4. If the feet of the animals are not included in the fabric as pictured, either cover the foot areas with clumps of flowers or foliage or add feet (hooves in this case) to the animal's legs with a black fabric marker.

Patch a zebra.

Holsteins

How could two Wisconsin quilters not make a cow quilt? Notice that the background we used is similar to the previous quilt, "Horses Out to Pasture." However, with the gentle cows nonchalantly chewing their cud, the mood of the quilt is very different.

You can create this design by following the directions for "Horses Out to Pasture," page 36. The choice of the conversational cow print is what gives this quilt a new focus. Notice, too, that this quilt has a playful border.

Note from NANCY

After I hinted to Natalie that most dairy farmers have only one breed of cow on their farm (being a farmer's daughter I know these things), Natalie chose only the Holstein cows and calves from this interesting fabric. Now she's making another quilt featuring Guernsey cows (or as she calls them, the "brown" cows) from the same fabric.

Elijah and Friends

"Elijah and Friends" was designed for a little boy who loves animals and nature but not the fences in zoos. We opened the garden gate and invited the animals into the backyard to play. Of course giraffes don't carry banners with names and zebras probably shouldn't eat the flowers, but thinking like a kid makes for livelier quilts.

Selecting Fabrics

1. Select a light blue summer sky fabric for the background fabric. We used a commercial fabric with subtle pale blue streaks.

2. Choose a groundcover fabric with multiple hues of green. If the fabric already has flowers in it, that's all the better. Include additional fabrics of small- to medium-scale floral prints. The flowers and grasses can be very childlike.

3. Select a wood-grain fabric for the fence posts.

4. Find interesting conversational prints of wild animals. Pay attention to the style and size of the animals, making certain the proportions and moods of the prints are compatible. Or use some of the *Landscape Animals* in the back of this book by transferring the images to printer fabric sheets.

"Elijah and Friends" fabric array.

Creating the Scene

Create the background.

1. Cut the sky background fabric the size of the finished quilt. The background in "Elijah and Friends" measures 42" x 25".

2. Messy cut the top of the groundcover fabric. The uneven terrain creates an interesting meadow. The grasslike fabric should cover approximately one-third of the background fabric.

3. Liberally glue and position the groundcover fabric to the bottom one-third of the background fabric. For gluing guidelines, see page 15.

4. Fussy cut the animals. Don't worry if the entire animal's body isn't included in the print (see Patching Animals, page 38). If the animal feet aren't included in the fabric, simply cover the foot area with a cluster of flowers.

If you can't find animals to your liking elsewhere, use the printer transfer images in the back of the book. You'll find zebras, a koala bear, a monkey, an elephant, and two friendly giraffes. Instructions for transferring the animals to printer fabric sheets are on page 17.

5. Spread glue on the wrong side of the animals and position them on the design.

6. Messy cut flowers from the floral fabric to resemble flower clusters. Glue and place flowers near the animals. Scatter the additional flowers throughout the quilt design.

7. Cut pickets for the fence 1" x 6". Round the top of the pickets by trimming off the corners.

8. Glue the pickets across the design, about 3" apart from each other, with the bottom of the posts about 5" from the bottom of the background fabric. We used 19 pickets and left a 6" space for the zebra to walk into the garden.

Transfer Landscape Animals to printer fabric sheets.

Position the animals.

Add the fence.

Create the gate.

Add more animals and flowers.

Felt craft letters and "make-your-own" letters.

9. Create a gate from five extra fence pickets.

a. Place two pickets wrong side up about 3" apart from each other.

b. Cut another picket in half lengthwise and use the two strips to form a top and bottom rail between the two reversed pickets. Glue them to the side pickets.

c. Form a crisscross with the two remaining pickets and glue them over the square gate frame you've just created.

d. Move the gate to your design and glue it in place along the fence so it looks open. You can make the gate "swing" by twisting the square slightly so the shape is a parallelogram.

10. Cover the bases of most of the posts with additional flowers and shrubbery.

11. Glue and position more animals in front of the fence. We made sure the animals that made it into the garden were friendly-looking.

12. Cut a length of yarn, string, or several strands of embroidery floss the length desired. Pin the yarn between the giraffes' mouths.

13. Add letters to the clothesline. Pictured are 3" felt letters, purchased from a craft store and several letters from the two Alphabet Appliqués provided on pages 91 to 96. Follow the instructions for Making Alphabet Appliqués on page 18. For the letters, choose bright fabrics that will stand out in the sky.

14. Position the letters along the clothesline. We connected only one edge of the letters to the clothesline so that they hang unevenly. It may be necessary to adjust the height of the clothesline to accommodate the letter positions. Glue the craft letters in place. If you made Alphabet Appliqués from the book, fuse the letters in place.

15. Hand stitch the ends of the clothesline to the giraffes' mouths. Remove the pins.

Note from NATALIE

If you would like to see other ways to display your child's name besides giraffes holding clotheslines, check the kids' quilts in Chapter 3. Some names are held by birds, some are suspended from branches, and some are simply floating in the air.

A slightly different version for Bethany.

Stitching and Squaring the Quilt Top

1. Machine stitch around the shapes. Refer to the directions on page 20.

2. Square the quilt top. See the directions on page 21.

Auditioning and Adding Borders

Audition border fabrics by folding the potential border fabric to a narrow width and pinning it alongside the quilt top. Decide which border best fits the mood and colors of the quilt.

1. Cut the border strips. The borders for this quilt are cut 3½" wide.

2. Add the borders. See the directions on pages 22 to 23.

Audition border fabrics.

Note from NANCY

When Natalie was my guest on *Sewing With Nancy* for a three-part series on *Landscape Quilts for Kids*, we described the step-by-step process of the "Elijah and Friends" quilt under different names – "Bethany and Friends" and "Tom and Friends." One of the charms of this quilt design is that it is as fitting for little girls as it is for little boys.

Chapter 3

If you ask children what they would most like to see in a quilt besides their names, their answer would likely be themselves in action, playing with their friends. That's what this chapter is all about – depicting the kids we love in fabric, doing what they love to do.

This chapter contains six step-by-step *Landscape Kids* scenes that are simple to do and can be adapted for any child's room. Because we know first hand that finding just the right kids in a commercial fabric is very difficult, we've created them for you. In the back of this book, you will find, on page 80, boy and girl faces of all races, hair colors, and styles. On pages 81 to 87 you'll find clothing suitable for all seasons of the year, and on pages 88 to 90 a wide variety of toys, pets, sports equipment, cowboy outfits, and even Halloween costumes. In addition, we've included two alphabets already mirror-imaged so you can easily create your child's name on your quilt.

We've also included in the front of this chapter the actual children's quilts that inspired this book. Natalie had created these for her grandchildren before the idea for this book was born and they served as inspirations for each of the step-by-step quilts we designed for this chapter.

Kids at Play

How the

"LEAH"

Leah's quilt was the very first of the *Landscape Quilts for Kids*. I had made patchwork baby quilts for Leah's big sisters, Esther and Rochel, but Leah had a bedroom of her own with three bare walls. What a great opportunity to make her a personalized landscape quilt!

Creating the landscape was the easy part. To make it childlike, I kept it very simple. I cut out some sticklike tree trunks and lollipop leaves over a baby blue sky and added them to a piece of flowered and grass-filled meadow fabric.

Adding kids and a name was more difficult. I found some cartoonlike kids in a fabric from my stash, but they were dressed all wrong. With some tracing paper, a pencil, and a few calicos, I changed their clothes into pretty dresses (see page 57 for directions on how to do this yourself). And after much searching, I found some letters in a catalog.

Leah's mom was, of course, very happy with her new baby's quilt. But now, she asked, what about Esther's and Rochel's walls? Could I make two more – enough

alike so they didn't get jealous of each other but different enough so they'd each feel special?

"Right," said Grandma Natalie. So I dug out the scraps of the old kid fabric. I had less than half a yard left and the fabric was more than seven years old. But I had enough for Esther's quilt, and even enough for Rochel's, a fall scene. Once I had finished these quilts, it seemed only fair to use the last three fabric kids for a quilt for my other daughter's son, Ben. Ben's quilt is a scene like Rochel's, only set in winter.

By now, I was hooked on making landscape quilts for kids. But I was out of kid fabrics and out of letters. Why, I wondered, couldn't this be easier? How I wished for some cute fabric kids with a choice of clothes and toys and some big 3" letters for names.

That's when the concept for this chapter took shape. Nancy was convinced that moms and grandmas everywhere would enjoy making quilts like this for their children if they had the right materials. And so, with you in mind, we set about creating them.

"Kids" Began

"ESTHER"

In Esther's quilt I went a step further in personalizing the kids. I made the two little girls and their baby sister resemble my actual granddaughters as closely as possible.

To personalize the little brown-haired girl holding the balloons to look like Esther, who adores wearing fancy dresses, I placed tissue paper over the child's clothes in the fabric and outlined a dress and tights. After cutting out the new shapes, I added details with a #2 pencil. I simply glued the new outfit over the old and trimmed away the parts of the original yellow slicker that were wider than the new outfit. The shoes were trickier – I had to draw them freehand. The light brown curls were easy – I colored them in with a brown fabric marker and outlined them with a Sharp permanent black pen.

The process was similar for the second little girl, Esther's big sister, Rochel. I gave her a new purple calico dress by using the same techniques I had used for Esther's dress, and then lengthened and darkened her hair with a black fabric marker. I had to draw freehand

baby Leah watching her sisters from her blanket nearby. (You will find a baby on a blanket to use in your quilts on page 83.) I cut out the balloons from a conversational print I found in my stash and purchased the felt letters that spell Esther's name from a craft store. As you can see, I used the same simple landscape scene for Esther's quilt that I had created for Leah's.

"ROCHEL"

For Rochel's quilt, I changed the season. Esther, Rochel, and their friends are raking leaves in the fall. Again we have the two big trees, now golden and brown. The kids have raked leaves into a huge pile, and when they finish jumping in them, will take them to the curb in their wagons and baskets. I found the wonderful Radio Flyer wagon in a conversational print that happened to be the right scale for the kids. The basket was hand drawn. (You will find a wagon and a basket to use for your quilts on page 84.)

I used the same fabric as the leaves to spell Rochel's name and scattered individual leaves over the background to look like they're falling.

"BEN"

Ben's quilt gave me a chance to depict winter and build a snowman. Three little kids are playing in the snow on a dark winter day. The trees are bare and little birds are helping to hold up the letters in Ben's name. (The snowman, the sled, and some terrific snowsuits are available on pages 85 and 88 for you to use in your quilts.)

Spring & Summer Scenes

Feel free to adapt the following scenes to make them reflect your child. Once you get comfortable with creating a quilt or two, we are sure you will want to take off on inventions of your own.

Anna

"Anna" is a good example of how you can customize a quilt for your child by using the kids, accessories, and letters from the back of the book. Anna's quilt features three children holding up the letters while a big sister plays with her baby sister nearby. If you look closely you'll see a dog studying a bird in the tree and another puppy making friends with the baby. All of these kids and pets, as well as the letters, are found on pages 80 to 96. Look through them to find the ones that look enough like your child to put on your quilt.

Notice how simple the landscape is. Like the scene in the "Leah" quilt on page 48, it features a sunny sky, two trees, and a meadow to play in. The trees are fat sticks with lollipop tops, not unlike a tree a child might draw. The groundcover is grass, a few rocks, and some flowers, much like a drawing a child would make. You'll see as the chapter proceeds that we use the same scene again and again in all kinds of weather and all hours of the day. It's an easy scene to create and it sets a nice big stage for the kids, their pets, and their toys.

Selecting Fabrics

1. For a spring or summer scene, choose a pale blue fabric for the sky. Pale blue allows the kids to be illuminated. If your fabric has a few puffy clouds and some rays of pink or yellow, all the better.

2. Choose grass or groundcover foliage prints that are small in scale with splashes of flowers. We added a few extra flowers from a second fabric for more color.

3. Select dark textured fabrics for the tree trunks. Brown, dark gray, and even black shades are suitable.

4. Choose leaf-print fabrics for the tree foliage that are small to medium scale. Having at least two hues of leaves makes the tree foliage more interesting.

5. Choose fabrics for the letters that convey the tone you want. Small-scale plaids, checks, or stripes are ideal for both boys' and girls' rooms; floral prints are great for girls. You may want to coordinate your fabrics with the color and style of the child's actual room. Make certain that the colors of the letters are not too pale against the light blue sky.

"Anna" fabric array.

Note: All the kids, clothing, pets, and accessories are found on pages 80 to 90 and can be transferred to printer fabric sheets.

Create the background and add tree trunks.

Creating the Scene

1. Cut the sky fabric the full size of the quilt. This one is 36" x 24".

2. Use a strip of groundcover fabric approximately one-third the height of the background and the same width. Messy cut the top edge of the fabric.

3. Liberally glue and position the groundcover fabric to the bottom third of the background fabric. (See the directions for gluing on page 15.)

4. Cut childlike tree trunks approximately 18" long x 1½" to 2" wide. Glue the wrong side of the fabric. Position the trees at least 1½" up from the bottom of the quilt. (See the directions for cutting trees, page 15.)

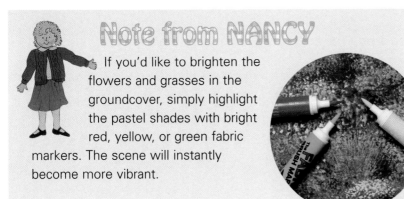

Note from NANCY

If you'd like to brighten the flowers and grasses in the groundcover, simply highlight the pastel shades with bright red, yellow, or green fabric markers. The scene will instantly become more vibrant.

5. Messy cut leaves for the trees, preferably from two coordinating fabrics. On our quilt, only one edge is messy cut, the other two edges form the top corners of the quilt top. Glue the wrong sides of the fabric and position them on the quilt top.

6. Give the tree trunks dimension by highlighting one side of the tree with a correction pen.

Adding the Children and the Name

1. Transfer the *Landscape Kids'* faces and the summer outfits to printer fabric sheets as described on pages 16 to 17.

2. Fussy cut the heads and bodies. Place a dab of glue on the base of the necks and attach the heads to the bodies.

Note from NANCY

Little kids have short necks. Experiment with the placement of the head on the body and the angle of the head. You can create interesting attitudes for these kids by simply tipping their heads slightly to the left or right.

3. Consider the number of letters in your child's name. It goes without saying that you'll need more children to hold up the name "Penelope" than you'll need for "Matt." As you are choosing the children's bodies, notice their arm positions. Make certain that the body position will allow you to spell the name comfortably. The letters certainly do not need to be held straight or even.

Note from NANCY

You may choose to have the letters held by birds or simply suspended in the sky. Glance through the other children's quilts in this chapter to see alternative ways of positioning letters.

4. Spread glue on the wrong sides of the children and position them in place. Glue or fuse the letters as well.

Stitching and Squaring the Quilt Top

1. Machine stitch around the shapes. Refer to the directions on page 20.
2. Square the quilt top. See the directions on page 21.

Auditioning and Adding the Borders

Audition border fabrics by folding the potential border fabric to a narrow width and pinning it alongside the quilt top. Decide which border best fits the mood and colors of the quilt.

1. Cut the border strips. The borders for this quilt were cut 3½" wide.
2. Add the borders. See the directions on pages 22 to 23.

Personalized Quilts

In this section, we'll show you how to change the kids' body positions, hairstyles, and clothes to personalize the quilts. This variety will, we hope, allow you to select the child who most closely resembles your own and the activities he or she loves best.

Jessica

The luxury of having so many choices of kids' faces, clothes, accessories, and pets is obvious when you look at the "Jessica" quilt. Although the scenery is again the two simple trees in the meadow, it's now ablaze with activity. The *Landscape Kids* are everywhere, playing with trucks in the sandbox, flying balloons, watering flowers, and playing with their dogs.

Changing Body Positions

The *Landscape Kids* have a variety of body positions. Some can hold letters, fly kites, or hold onto horses while riding bareback. However, you may want them to do your kid's favorite activity or something else. You can easily modify the stance of the cutout child by cutting along the armhole of the garment, repositioning the arm, and adding, if necessary, a small snippet of like-colored fabric in the newly created space. A dab of glue will temporarily hold the repositioned piece. Later in the quilting stage, the pieces will be securely stitched and no one will be the wiser.

Change the arm position.

Create a kneeling child.

This picture of Nancy's nephew, Ethan, playing in a sandbox, was one of the inspirations for this quilt. To depict a child kneeling in the quilt just like the child in the photo, we simply cut off the *Landscape Kid*'s legs at the knee and placed a dump truck in front of him.

Note from NATALIE

Here's a photo of Rochel with her very distinctive long dark hair and bangs. Here's the face that most closely resembles hers. Here's the new *Landscape Kid* Rochel, thanks to the magic of fabric markers. I'm sure she will recognize herself.

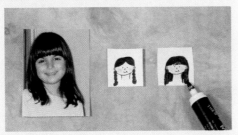

Changing the Hairstyle

If you can't find your child's hairstyle among the options on page 80, you can modify the hairstyle that comes closest to your child's with the magic of fabric-marking pens. After transferring the faces to Printer Fabric Sheets, cut out the face that most closely resembles your child's. Draw longer hair, add bangs and curls, or even add color highlights.

Change a child's clothes.

Personalizing Clothing

Remember paper dolls? With the magic of scissors, a paper doll's outfit could change simply by placing a new one on top of it. You can do the same thing with these kids. By following a few short steps, a *Landscape Kid* dressed in shorts and a tank top can be dressed in a sundress of your making.

Note from NANCY

The scale of design in the fabrics for little girl's dresses is so important. Use the tiniest of calico prints for the new clothes. Anything larger will look inappropriate.

1. Place tissue paper or a quilting template such as Templar over the *Landscape Kid*.
2. Draw the outline of the new outfit. Then trace it onto the dress fabric you have chosen.
3. Cut out the new outfit. Add details such as buttons, ruffles, or zippers by simply sketching with a #2 pencil.
4. Glue the new outfit onto the *Landscape Kid*.

A Horse of My Own

A similar scene with a grassy meadow, clear sky, and a big oak-like tree make up the background for this delightful quilt. By adding a fence, a few horses, and some horse tack, you can turn a scene like that in Anna's or Jessica's quilt into "A Horse of My Own."

Note from NATALIE

One of my grandsons has been passionate about horses for two years and he's only three years old! I couldn't resist creating a scene that would depict his fondest dreams. As soon as he saw it, he knew he was the one riding bareback. Then he proceeded to name all his preschool friends – "That's Allison on the other horse, that's Nathan with the pets. That's Zoe patting my horse, that's Sean carrying the pail and rope . . ." Unintentionally, I admit, our *Landscape Kids* looked like his friends. I couldn't have been happier.

Create the fence with a fabric marker.

Highlight the fence with a white correction pen.

Creating the Scene

1. Create a background with a clear sky fabric, grassy meadow, tree, and additional shrubbery pieces. Follow the guidelines as detailed in the "Anna" quilt on pages 52 to 55 but feel free to vary the background.

2. Create the fence by drawing directly on the fabric with fabric markers and a correction pen. You might want to experiment on a scrap of fabric first.

a. Use a black marking pen to draw fence posts approximately 3" apart.

b. Draw crosswise rails to connect the posts.

c. Highlight the posts and rails with a white correction pen.

3. Fussy cut the horses and kids from printer fabric sheets. Assemble the kids as described on page 54. Glue and position the kids, horses, and tack to the scene.

Transfer the horse and horse accessories to a printer fabric sheet.

Note from NANCY

To enable a *Landscape Kid* to ride bareback on the horse, pick a body with the legs together and facing slightly left with the knees slightly bent. Cut the legs apart up to the crotch area. Slip the child on the horse to assume a riding position and position the horse and riders on the scene. Natalie used horses from a commercial fabric but you can also use the horse and accessories found on page 90.

Fall & Winter Scenes

To change the scene to fall or winter, simply select new background fabrics and choose kids wearing warmer clothes or snowsuits (pages 81 to 85).

Joey

Autumn sets the tone in this red and gold scene featuring Joey and his *Landscape Kids* friends. We created this quilt to highlight all the wonderful fall outfits and accessories available to you. The landscape scene is almost identical to Rochel's quilt on page 50, but the kids, their rakes, and their pets are simply a printer and a scissors away.

Note from NATALIE

I couldn't resist extending part of the scene into the border. Look at the dogs in each bottom corner and the leaves on the right side of the quilt. After sewing the borders to the scene, I just glued and stitched them outside the line!

Selecting Fabrics

1. Select a sky fabric for the background fabric. For a fall scene, the sky can be streaked with blues and grays.

2. Choose several fall-like groundcover fabrics ranging from green to gold and brown in color. We used three fabrics for the groundcover.

3. Select a medium-scale fall leaf print for the foliage on the trees.

4. Select a dark wood bark fabric for the trees.

"Joey" fabric array.

Creating the Scene

1. Cut the sky fabric the full size of the quilt background. This one is 32" x 20".

2. Cut two to three mounds of groundcover fabric approximately one-third the height of the background. Overlap the edges of the mounds to create the piles of leaves. Messy cut the curved areas of each mound.

3. Liberally glue, overlap, and position the groundcover fabric to the bottom third of the background fabric. For gluing guidelines, see page 15.

Create the background and the trees.

Add the letters, the children, and their accessories.

4. Cut child-like tree trunks, approximately 18" long x 1½" to 2" wide. Glue the wrong side of the fabric. Position the trees at least 1½" to 2" up from the bottom of the quilt. (See tree cutting guidelines on page 15).

5. Messy cut leaves for the trees. Only one edge needs to be messy cut since the other two edges form the top corners of the quilt top. Glue the wrong sides of the leaf fabric and position them on the quilt top.

6. Transfer the children's faces and the fall outfits of your choice to printer fabric sheets as described on page 17.

7. Fussy cut the heads and bodies. Place a dab of glue on the base of the neck and attach the head to the body.

8. Spread glue on the wrong sides of the children and position them in place.

9. Cut, glue, and add the accessories such as wagons, baskets, rakes, pets, etc. Most of these can be found on page 84. Or you may want to cut out accessories from other commercial conversational prints.

10. Using the Alphabet Appliqué technique on page 18, cut out the letters of your child's name and place them in the sky. Either fuse or glue them into place.

11. Fussy cut single leaves, then glue them to the background as if they were falling from the trees.

Stitching and Squaring the Quilt Top

1. Machine stitch around the shapes. Refer to the directions on page 20.

2. Square the quilt top. See the directions on page 21.

Auditioning and Adding the Borders

1. Audition border fabrics and cut border strips. The borders for this quilt are 3½" wide.

2. Add the borders. See the directions on pages 22 to 23.

Halloween

A fter we finished the "Joey" quilt, we couldn't resist the temptation to change the time of day to evening and create a Halloween quilt. We also thought it would be fun to create a holiday decoration quilt as well as a child's wall quilt.

Selecting Fabrics

The only differences between "Joey" and "Halloween" are the dark sky and kids dressed in costumes. For the evening sky, choose either a hand-dyed or commercially-dyed batik navy. For fabric selection and design guidelines, follow the step-by-step directions given for "Joey" on page 60.

As for the costumes themselves, you'll see a wide variety on pages 86 and 87. Notice that we used the ghost costume twice and tilted one of them differently from the other, and we couldn't resist making the superhero a little girl.

From summer to fall, the fabric shops are full of Halloween prints. Add pumpkins, scarecrows, skeletons, bats, etc. The only caution is to avoid objects that are either too big or too small in scale for the children. Notice that the two dogs and many of the pumpkins are from conversational fabrics.

Since the word, "Halloween," would be too long to spell on the quilt, we shortened it to "Boo!" We cut the letters out of a fall grass fabric.

Halloween conversational prints.

Peace

Converting a snowy scene to a Christmas scene was easy. We already had the kids and their snowsuits and earlier had created a snowy landscape (see "Ben" on page 51). Now all we needed were a few fir trees, Christmas tree trimmings, and some musical equipment to make a children's outdoor holiday scene. As you can see, four kids are trimming a tree, three are singing carols, and one is pulling her puppy to join them. All the kids, their clothes, and accessories are available to you on pages 80 to 90.

Selecting Fabrics

1. Select a dark navy for the background fabric. We used a navy hand-dyed fabric for the cold winter sky. An attractive commercial fabric such as a navy or royal blue batik would be another effective choice. Make sure your winter sky fabric has mottled hues and avoid using solid colors.

2. Choose a multi-hued light gray print for the snow fabric. Snow never appears as a solid white. It always has shadows of gray, blue, and cream, depending on the light in the sky.

3. Choose a medium to dark tree trunk fabric. Ours is multi-shades of gray to brown.

4. Select a multi-shaded green fabric for making several fir trees. Our quilt has four.

"Peace" fabric array.

5. Check at a craft or fabric store for sequins on a string as well as separate sequins to serve as ornaments on the tree.

6. Select fabric(s) for the letters that spell "PEACE." We added a snow fabric double for all the letters to make sure they were legible against the dark sky.

Note: In addition to our winter and holiday accessories on pages 85 and 88, look for holiday prints at fabric stores. The fabrics pictured show just a sampling of the many holiday elements you could add to your quilt.

Holiday conversational prints.

Creating the Scene

1. Cut the sky background fabric the size of the finished quilt. This background measures 29" x 21".

2. Messy cut the top of the snow, creating a gentle hill. The uneven terrain adds interest to the simple scene. The snow section should cover the bottom third of the background fabric.

3. Position and glue the snow fabric to the lower edge of the background fabric. For gluing guidelines, see page 15.

4. Cut one tree from the tree fabric. Vary the width of the trunks to add interest. Cut the bottom of the tree trunks jagged to make the base of the tree look snow-covered. Glue and position the trees to the background.

5. Cut branches from thin strips of the tree fabric and spread glue on the backs. When positioning the branches on the fabric, give the branches "elbows" rather than curves.

6. If the tree trunks are too dark against the background, lighten one side with a white marker or correction pen (see page 54).

7. Add a few fir trees to the scene. Find a fir tree template on page 75.

Create the background and trees.

Position the cardinals on branches.

Cut double letters and offset them.

Fabric markers turn the kids into carolers.

Add the Christmas tree trim.

8. Cut and glue cardinals to the branches. Find cardinal images on page 88.

9. Using the Alphabet Appliqué technique on page 18, cut double letters for "PEACE" and slightly offset them. Position and fuse the letters to the background to make it appear as if the cardinals are holding the corners of the letters.

10. Transfer the children, holiday accessories, and Christmas decorations to printer fabric sheets, as described on pages 16 to 17. Fussy cut, glue, and position the kids on the scene.

11. Change the kids into carolers by turning their smiling mouths into ovals. We simply added a little circle to the bottom of their smiles with a black permanent ink pen, and presto, their mouths were open to sing.

12. Hand stitch the sequin "garland" and individual sequins to the Christmas tree.

Stitching and Squaring the Quilt Top

1. Machine stitch around the shapes. Refer to the directions on page 20.

2. Square the quilt top. See page 21 for directions.

Auditioning and Adding Borders

1. Audition border fabrics and cut border strips. The borders for this quilt were cut wide.

2. Refer to the directions on pages 22 to 23 to add the borders.

Digital Photo

1. Transfer the original photo to fabric.
2. Cut the child out from the fabric photo.
3. Position the child on the landscape quilt top.

By using an actual photo of your child or grandchild, you can create his or her exact image in a wall quilt. The process is as simple as using our drawings. Simply print your photo onto printer fabric, cut out the child or children you want to use, then glue and position them on your fabric landscape scene.

Creating the Scene

In both "Esther Goes Fishing" and "Rochel Climbs a Tree" we re-created very similar landscapes to the ones in the original photographs.

Esther is standing on the bank of a pond, pretending to fish. We gave her a real fishing pole. Rochel really climbed a tree branch that was only a few feet off the ground. We made the trunk's branches much higher to show what a great climber she is.

In both scenes, we greatly simplified the backgrounds and left out many details. We were able to find a green fabric that actually changes hue from dark to light, which gave us an easy way to re-create grass. You can achieve a similar look by either

Transfer Quilts

using the back of the fabric as well as the front, or creating a lighter shade of grass with markers. Or you can change the scene to feature shrubs and foliage instead of lawn.

In "Rochel Climbs a Tree," we were careful to re-create the same tree shape in fabric as existed in the original photograph so that her hands and body would look natural on the new tree. We simply traced, with tracing paper or a template, the part of the tree she was climbing on, then extended the rest of the tree trunk and branches to enlarge the tree.

Be cautious when machine quilting the actual fabric photo. We found that even extra thin machine needles create unsightly holes in the dense photo transfer fabric. Quilt as little as possible on the bodies and faces of the children themselves. We stitched on the edges to hold them firmly in place but did almost no quilting on their hair and faces.

1. Transfer the original photo to fabric.
2. Cut the child out from the fabric photo.
3. Position the child on the landscape quilt top.

Chapter 4

Now that you have created a landscape quilt top for your child, you're ready for the finishing touches. This chapter covers some basic techniques for layering your quilt and free-motion stitching. We'll also discuss some easy tips for quilting borders, making a sleeve, and creating a special label for a quilt that your child will treasure. Last, but not least, we'll show you how to block your quilt so it hangs flat on the wall.

Left: "Kids Flying Kites" was one of the earliest Landscape Kid quilts. It's much like a child's drawing – huge blue sky, grass filled with flowers, and little kids at play. If you look closely, you'll see some animals hidden in the grasses.

Finishing Your Quilt

Layering Your Quilt

Choose a backing fabric that fits the mood of your scene. It doesn't need to be one of the fabrics used in the quilt, but your child will love having a print that carries out the mood of the quilt top. For example, on our cow quilts we used a backing that features farm animals. On our zebra quilts, we used a jungle print. We even backed some of our kid quilts with whimsical flannels that matched their bed sheets or other room décor.

The backing of both the cow and zebra quilts.

1. Place the backing fabric wrong-side-up on a flat surface such as a table. Secure the backing to the surface with masking tape. Give the corners a little tug, stretching them gently so the backing is completely smooth. This helps eliminate puckers as you machine quilt.

2. Select a lightweight batting. We used Pellon Polyester Fleece, but there are many other lightweight batts that work well for wall hangings. Place the batting on top of the backing fabric and smooth it out with your hands. Then place the quilt top on the batting, right side up.

3. Pin the layers of the quilt together with safety pins, spacing the pins about 3" apart. Use your fist as a measuring guide when spacing the pins. The pins should be no further apart than your fist. This adequately secures the layers, yet won't interfere with the machine quilting.

4. Roll the quilt toward the center from each short end. Secure the rolled section with pins or quilts clips.

Free-Motion Quilting

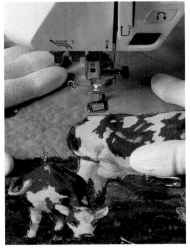

Close-up of the tight free-motion quilting in the sky.

We recommend using free-motion quilting to secure the three layers of your quilt together. It's enjoyable once you get comfortable with doing it, and it gives your quilt texture and personality. For those unfamiliar with free-motion quilting, here are some simple guidelines.

- Lower the feed dogs and attach a darning foot.
- Begin the free-motion quilting at the center of your piece and work out toward the borders.
- Complete the entire landscape scene before you begin the borders.
- Wear rubber fingers, quilting gloves, or use a Quilt Sew Easy hoop to be able to grip the fabric effectively as you sew (see page 13).
- Sew at a medium to fast speed and move the fabric at a slow speed.
- Remove the safety pins one-by-one as you go along.
- Reroll the fabric as you complete quilting in one area.
- The same quilting intensity should extend over the entire quilt surface. If you've quilted intensely in the center of the quilt, you will have to do the same in the rest of the scene and in the border. If your border is not quilted as heavily as the body it will pucker and look ruffled. Intense quilting takes up a lot of fabric inches!
- Experiment with various quilting options. When you free-motion quilt areas of sky, you can create clouds by leaving small areas unquilted. The unquilted areas will appear to come forward in the design.

Close-up of free-motion quilting.

Note: *If you prefer not to quilt intensely, you may simply outline quilt the pieces down to hold the quilt sandwich together. Outline quilting is minimal free-motion quilting, which works especially well on simple quilts that have very few elements, such as "Horses Out to Pasture." In large areas like the sky, simply run quilt lines across the scene.*

Note from NATALIE

When I free-motion quilt around the faces of children made from printer fabric sheets, I do as little quilting as possible. Because the transferred fabric is very dense, the sewing machine needle leaves holes. I use a size 70 sharp needle to minimize the problem.

Finishing Techniques

Now that you've free-motion stitched the entire scene of your landscape quilt, it's time to finish the quilt by stitching the borders, adding the binding, adding a sleeve, blocking, and labeling your quilt.

Stitching the Borders

Stitch in the ditch on the seam between the border and your scene to create a mat line. This easy step stabilizes the quilt and gives it a finished look. Then add free-motion quilting to the remaining border area, and your quilt is nearly complete.

1. Raise the feed dogs and engage or attach the dual feed or walking foot to your sewing machine.

2. Attach a conventional presser foot.

3. Use the same needle and thread combination that you used for free-motion quilting the body of your quilt.

4. Stitch in the ditch, sewing along the seam between the quilt scene and the border. This defines one edge of the simulated mat.

5. Form the second edge of the mat by stitching in the border ¼" or a presser foot width away from the first stitching. Stitch a second line. This double stitching stabilizes the rectangle of your quilt design.

6. Add free-motion quilting to the remaining border areas. See page 71 for instructions.

Binding Your Quilt

A binding adds a finishing touch to the edges of your quilt. Follow these instructions to make a ½" double fold French binding.

1. Cut and join 2¼" wide crosswise strips with right sides together, using diagonal seams to reduce bulk. Join enough strips to equal the outer measurement of the quilt plus 6" to 8".

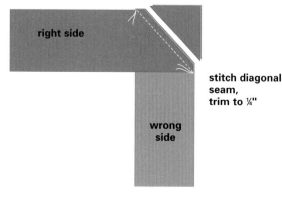

right side

stitch diagonal seam, trim to ¼"

wrong side

2. Cut the end of the strip at a 45º angle. Fold in ¼" at one short end of the binding. Fold the binding in half, wrong-sides-together, meeting the lengthwise edges. Press.

3. Meet the cut edges of the binding to the quilt top, beginning at the center of one edge of the quilt, right sides together. Mark the quilt top a scant ¼" from each corner.

4. Stitch the binding to the quilt top with a scant ¼" seam, beginning 4" from the end of the binding and stopping at the marked point at the first corner. Lock the stitches.

5. Fold the binding up at a 45° angle, aligning the cut edge of the binding with the cut edge of the quilt.

6. Fold the binding down, meeting the binding fold to the top edge of the quilt and the binding cut edges to the quilt side edges.

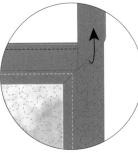

7. Stitch a scant ¼" seam on the side, starting at the folded edge.

8. Repeat at the remaining corners, stopping 3" to 4" before the start of the binding. Insert the free end of the binding inside the beginning of the binding so the binding is smooth and even with the quilt. Trim away the excess binding if necessary. Stitch the remainder of the binding seam.

9. Fold the binding to the wrong side, covering the stitching line and tucking in the corners to form miters.

10. Hand stitch the folded edge of the binding to the quilt backing.

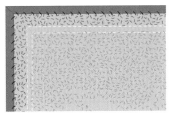

Blocking

Blocking your landscape quilt is an important step in creating an effective wall hanging. No matter how careful your craftsmanship has been every step of the way, inevitably a corner of your quilt will curl a little or a section will buckle. Blocking your quilt on a vertical surface with plenty of hot steam will convince your wall hanging to lie flat against the wall and behave. If you don't have a vertical surface, use any flat surface available to you. Blocking gives the entire quilt a finished look.

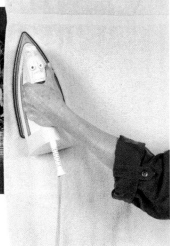

Block your quilt.

1. Using a small damp hand towel, cover a section of the quilt.

2. Press the quilt through the towel with a hot iron. The process should provide plenty of steam.

3. Move the damp towel to the next area of the quilt. Rewet the towel if necessary. Press.

4. Pin the bottom corners flat and measure to make sure the quilt is hanging as it should.

5. Allow the quilt to dry overnight.

Adding a Hanging Sleeve

A hanging sleeve lets you display your quilt on a wall after it has been completed. The sleeve described below allows the quilt to hang parallel to the wall without buckling or pulling down the corners.

1. Cut an 8" strip of fabric 1" shorter than the width of the quilt.

2. Turn under ¼" at both short ends of the strip.

3. Fold the strips right sides together, meeting the lengthwise edges.

4. Stitch a ¼" seam along the lengthwise edge.

5. Turn the tube right side out and press.

6. Center the tube on the upper edge of the quilt, positioning the tube ½" from the top. Hand stitch along the lower fold.

7. Fold back the sleeve ½" from the top fold. Hand stitch the sleeve to the quilt, catching only the first layer of fabric.

8. Insert a rod that is slightly narrower than the width of the quilt.

Labeling Your Quilt

Your finished quilt, which most likely is a gift to a beloved child, deserves a label. There are many fancy ways to label a quilt, but here's a simple, quick way that conveys the information you need to provide and also maintains the mood you created in your landscape quilt.

1. Select a 6" to 8" square piece of light-colored fabric that coordinates with the backing fabric.

2. Press under ¼" along all four sides of the square.

3. Cut out and glue a few motifs such as you used on the front of your quilt in one of the corners of the fabric square. For example, if your quilt features panda bears, a panda or two would be perfect.

4. Free-motion stitch the motifs to the label fabric.

5. With a permanent marker, write your quilt's name, your name, and the date on the label square. You may want to add the recipient's name and the occasion for the gift, such as, "For James, on his 11th birthday."

6. Hand-appliqué your label to the lower right-hand corner of the quilt's backing.

Glue and stitch motifs to the label.

The back of a finished quilt.

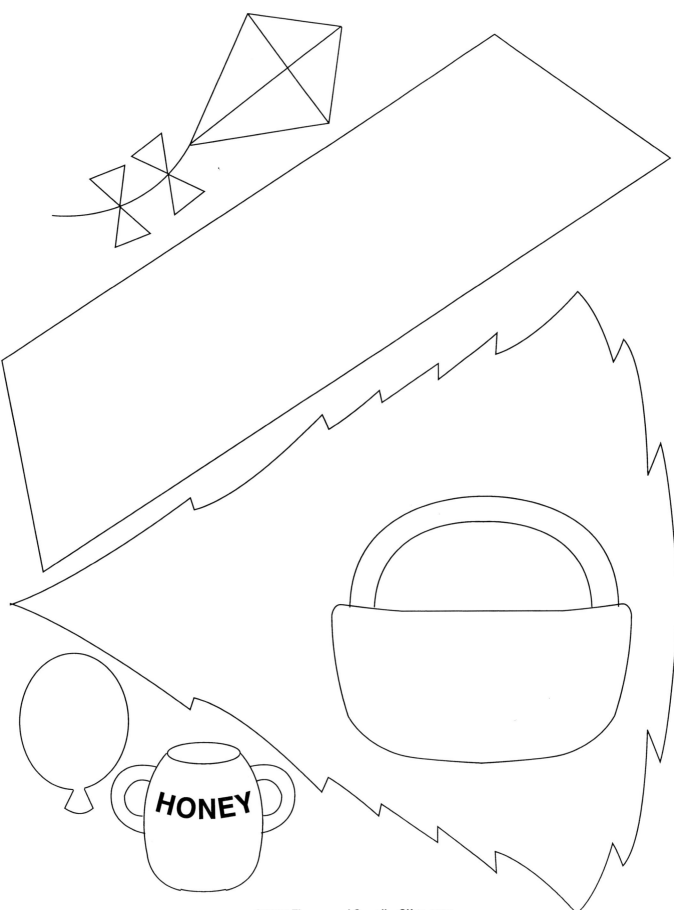

HONEY

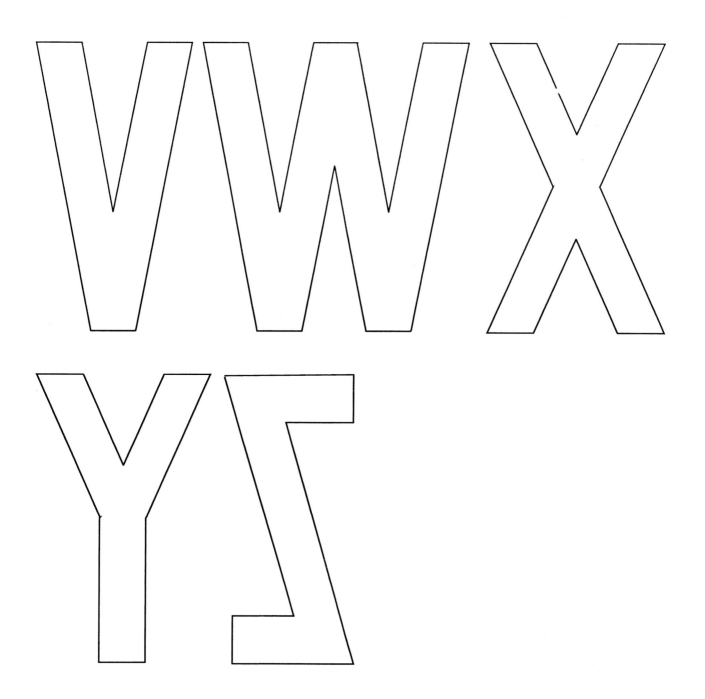